Barbara Willard

The Dragon Box

Illustrated by George Buchanan

Macdonald Children's Books

If only there were just a little less of him, Thomas thought, it would be wonderful to see him.

There was so much to talk about, and it took so much time to show Uncle Ned his room, and his clothes tidy in the chest of drawers, and his suits hanging in the cupboard with his boots and shoes in a neat row beneath, that the welcome home feast was still going on at past five o'clock that evening.

Florence bustled round the table, urging Uncle Ned to another piece of chicken, another slice of ham, just a spoonful more potato. She cut generously into the apple pie, which must have been one of the best she had ever made, for its crust was like flakes of gold. She pressed the jug of cream into Uncle Ned's hands.

"You'll ruin me, Florence! Don't you know I've been ill once already, or I wouldn't be where I am today."

"You're over it," she assured him. "I never saw you looking bonnier, Mr Ned, and I've known you, man and boy, for all of forty years." And she wheedled him – "Another crumb of this fine Stilton, sir? A drop more port wine?"

"You'll build me up to twice my size, Florence," he said, groaning. "Anyone will tell you I'm quite big enough as it is. What do you say, young Thomas?"

Thomas was sitting there chewing the last mouthful of his apple pie. Somehow he could not get rid of it, so he only nodded.

He had been quite unable to speak all this time, for he was torn in two by his feelings. Uncle Ned was so huge that he was also hugely kind – and that showed in his twinkling eyes and the way his big voice softened.

But Thomas was waiting for something, waiting all the time. He was waiting for Uncle Ned to speak of the Dragon Box, and how it must be unlocked, and what it contained...

It was not until Uncle Ned had drunk a second glass of port and lighted a little black cigar that the moment came.

"There's a fine carpet for you, Mary, in that great parcel of sacking," he told his sister. "Take my knife and get to opening it. Thomas and I have other things to see to. The Dragon Box has arrived safely, I observe."

The chewed apple pie settled itself in Thomas's left cheek.

"Is my present in there, Uncle Ned?"

"For sure it is." Uncle Ned had pulled out the other end of his watch-chain and there dangled a key that looked as if it might be made of silver. He twiddled the key on the end of its chain, tilting back his chair a little, closing one eye against the smoke curling from his cigar.

"Shall we go and open the box, young Thomas?"

Thomas swallowed at last. "What's in it?"

"Now what would you expect to find in such a box?" Uncle Ned demanded.

"A dragon?" said poor Thomas, in a wobbly voice.

"That's certainly what I'd expect myself," agreed Uncle Ned. And he laughed enormously.

Thomas slid from his chair. He sidled out of the room and closed the door behind him. He was in the hall, with the Dragon Box on the floor at his side and the front door ahead of him. He ran to the front door and opened it, tugging because it was heavy, and then he was outside in the street. He ran.

Chapter Four

The spring day had died away into dusk and the sky was misted. The lamplighter was walking down the street with his long pole over his shoulder. One by one as he passed and touched them with the pole, the lamps came magically to life and shone through the twilight like so many golden moons.

Someone shouted, "Hi, Thomas! Young Thomas, hi!"

Thomas ran on, with Uncle Ned behind him striding easily.

Thomas got a terrible stitch in his side, and he stopped, groaning.

Uncle Ned stopped, too. He did not rush at Thomas and grab him, but stood several paces away.

"What's up with you, you silly lad?" he muttered, almost to himself.

Thomas shivered. His teeth chattered. He could not speak.

"You're not frightened of me, are you?" Uncle Ned cried, dismay and unhappiness in his face.

"No!" cried Thomas, surprised to find that this was true. "No, no! Oh no! *No*!"

"But frightened of something, eh? Come on, then. Tell me. Tell me what. Two heads are better than one. We'll face it together."

"The dragon," Thomas said, almost wailing.

Uncle Ned said nothing for a moment. They stood staring at one another, he and Thomas, and Thomas saw one thought after another change the expression on his uncle's big face.

"Better come home," said Uncle Ned at last. "It's chilly out here, and you've got to be brave. I'll help you all I can."

He held out his hand and slowly, very slowly, Thomas put his own into it. Uncle Ned's hand was big and it was hard, as might be expected, but it was also very warm. It was a good thing to hang on to, Thomas decided.

A little short of home, Uncle Ned stopped and looked down at Thomas.

"I'll tell you what," he said. "If you'd rather, we needn't open the Dragon Box at all. It can stay tight closed for as long as you wish – for always, if need be. I'll give you the key to hide or throw away. All the same, it would be better to see if the dragon's as bad as you think. For to tell the truth, Thomas, they hardly ever are."

They went into the house together, and there was the box. No one was about, for Mamma and Florence were in the parlour, unrolling the Chinese carpet from its wrappings and crying out in excitement at the colour and the pattern.

"Well?" said Uncle Ned to Thomas.

"Open it," said Thomas.

"Take the key. Open it for yourself, if you really want to."

"Don't go away," said Thomas.

He took the key that Uncle Ned had unhooked from his watch-chain. His fingers fumbled at the keyhole, but at last the key slid home and nothing remained but for Thomas to turn it and fling open the lid.

"You can still change your mind," Uncle Ned told him.

Thomas glanced at him very quickly. Why had he ever minded that he was so big and booming? If he were not, then he would be someone different, and not Thomas's Uncle Ned at all. And that, there was no doubt of it, would be a pity...

As he thought that, Thomas quickly flung up the lid of the Dragon Box. Then he opened his eyes, that he had squeezed shut. He saw that the box was crammed with all manner of things. But the dragon was on top.

"Take it," said Uncle Ned.

Thomas took the dragon out of the box carefully and using both hands. He looked at it slowly and for a long minute – at its beautiful bright colours and its fiery eyes, at its long twisting tail with the green and silver scales, at its wings, folded flat to its side just now, but ready all the same to fly.

“A kite!” said Thomas at last. “A dragon kite,” he said, his voice squeaking. “A dragon from the Land of the Dragon. It’s mine. It’s a dragon of my own – my very own dragon – isn’t it, Uncle Ned?”

“Have you flown a kite before?”

“Not ever.”

“Good. Then I can teach you. That’ll be fun for me, too.”

“Tomorrow?”

“If the wind’s right.”

“Morning,” said Thomas firmly.

“Morning it is.”

Thomas stood a second longer. He was beside himself with excitement, and with the beauty of the dragon which already in his imagination he saw sailing above the trees in the park. How the tail would lash, how the wings would spread – this was the most wonderful present he had ever been given. How dreadful it would be if he had no Uncle Ned to bring him such a gift from the far ends of the earth...

Suddenly his excitement burst out of him. He went stamping and shouting into the parlour, yelling out in a big boastful voice:

"I was right! I was right! There *was* a dragon in the Dragon Box!"

He saw Florence looking at him, the light glinting on her round, mended spectacles, so that he could not see her eyes.

"I told you!" cried Thomas.

PRINTED IN BELGIUM BY
proost
INTERNATIONAL BOOK PRODUCTION